# TAYLOR MADE

# TAYLOR MADE

## MY LIFE, MY STORY

## DR. WILL HARRIS

J MERRILL

J Merrill Publishing, Inc.
434 Hillpine Drive
Columbus, OH 43207
www.JMerrill.pub

Library of Congress Control Number: 2024906595
ISBN-13: 978-1-961475-21-2 (Paperback)
ISBN-13: 978-1-961475-29-8 (Hardcover)
ISBN-13: 978-1-961475-22-9 (eBook)
ISBN-13: 978-1-961475-30-4 (Audiobook)

Book Title: Taylor Made: My Life, My Story
Author: Dr. Will Harris
Editing: Veronica Fly
Cover Art: Vincent Tharpe/EmptyMe Graphic Design

*This book is dedicated to the memory of my mother, Mrs. Alean Toles Harris. I also dedicate this book to the millions of lives around the globe affected by mental illness.*

*None of this would be possible if it were not for my amazing Aunt Bonnie, who stepped in to cover and to raise me. I will never forget the many sacrifices you made to ensure that I would be a productive person in the world.*

*I am grateful for every teacher and every musical mentor who has poured into my life: Mrs. Gaye Calhoun, Mrs. Peggy Tubbs, Minister Billy Rivers, Dr. Leo Davis, Jr., the late Zebedee Reynolds Jones, Kurt Carr, Lamar Campbell, the late Dr. Anthony Stinson, James O. Pope Jr., Dr. Diane White-Clayton, Ira B. Wolfe, Dr. Sharon Cooper Brooks, A. Louise Lassiter, and my friends and fans all over the world who continue to support the gift in me.*

*Finally, I dedicate this book to every young person who has a dream, yet the circumstances surrounding you don't look promising. Keep dreaming, put your faith into motion, and make your dreams become a reality.*

# Contents

# FOREWORD BY
# M.LAMAR
# CAMPBELL

I am gospel recording artist, Lamar Campbell, most known for the song, "MORE THAN ANYTHING" which was named one of the top 100 gospel songs of all times by *Root Magazine*. I am honored to share from my perspective why I believe in the author, Will Harris and this amazing book. From an artist/song writer's point of view, there are key elements that we look for in a body of work that engage and stimulate us to want more. *Taylor Made* has what it takes to make this book hard to put down once you start the read.

Reading this book, you will feel the passion of someone who has not let his circumstances define him on his quest to truly getting to know himself in an honest way, from flaws to triumphs. It explores how our differences can be used to unite us as opposed to dividing us.

I am praying that as you read this book, it will inspire you to take an introspective look at your personal journey; and that it will catapult you into your greater you. This inspirational reality story has helped me reevaluate the importance of knowing that everything we go through leads to destiny. We determine the altitude of the destination by our belief system and what we feed our spirits. Congratulations Dr. Will Harris on your first book. May all those who read this book see the light inside of you that is in each one of us.

# PROLOGUE

C hasing destiny and purpose with no real sense of direction, guidance, and most importantly, no real knowledge of self-awareness can lead to layers of frustration and confusion. My mere existence here on earth is a miracle. Yet, from the very beginning, it was rooted in secrecy and denial. Those secrets kept me in a whirlwind of "wonder" for most of my life. As a child, I knew that success wouldn't come easy, and with the hand that I had been dealt, any level of success would require an incredible amount of strength and perseverance.

I didn't have the beautiful experience of being brought into the world by loving parents who were excited about my arrival. Neither did I have a family or a community that truly nurtured and celebrated me as a kid. I was simply the child of a mentally unstable parent that no one knew anything about until I was brought home from the hospital.

In my adult life, I began to see how my life was spinning out of control in a fight to understand why God would allow me to exist on earth and be born into such chaos. On most days, I felt that my only purpose on earth was to inspire and uplift others with my gift of music. While music ministry has always been fulfilling, I still struggled to understand why it always seemed that I was pouring my heart and soul into others through music, and no one was pouring back into me. I struggled to see that the hand of God has always been active in my life. It simply just wasn't manifesting itself in the ways for which I had dreamed and hoped.

In my journey of self-discovery, I learned that my purpose is far beyond my musical gifts and talents. My purpose is multifaceted. When I finally sat still and removed myself from the noise, I learned that I really didn't know who I was. I began to ask myself the question: Who am I? My response: I am God's child, a spiritual being having a human experience. That's who I am. I then asked myself: What do I want? My response: I want to achieve all that God had in mind when He created me. I want to live out the greatest manifestation of myself as a human being, and I want to reach my highest potential. This is what I want. Once I made this discovery, I realized that I could not move my life forward with no real sense of self. I had to do the tough work of deep self-reflection so that I could fully live out my true purpose and calling in life. In full transparency, this is "life work," and this work will never be completed. I have learned something new about myself each day since starting. Each day, there are more insights, and as I continue to pull back the layers, I've discovered that I will always be a flawed, imperfect human being with a willingness to better myself each day.

This book is a testament to the awesome power of God. My story is a story that mirrors mental dysfunction, strength, courage, perseverance, and resilience. God has designed each of us with a distinct DNA and a purpose in life that no one else can fulfill but us. There are millions around the globe who have similar callings and giftings, but no one does it the way you have been designed to do it. I have been gifted with a musical gift that neither my mother nor father displayed. For years, serving others through music was my greatest joy. I am now honored to step into another facet of my purpose and share the story of my life; in hopes that this book serves humanity and ministers to the core of someone else around the world.

## QR CODES

As you delve into this book, you'll encounter QR codes that link directly to songs I've written, performed, and produced. These codes are more than just a bridge between my story and my music; they are an invitation to experience the soundtrack of my journey, Dr. Will Harris.

Each QR code connects to a song that highlights key moments and reflections shared within these pages, from the inception of "Will Harris and Friends" to the various milestones that have marked my career. This integration of music and narrative offers a deeper understanding of my artistic journey and the evolution of my musical style.

I encourage you to scan these codes and let the music accompany you as you read. Through them, you'll gain insights into the power of faith, the importance of perseverance, and the pursuit of excellence that have defined my path.

Enjoy the immersive experience of story and song, and may it inspire and resonate with you.

# GOD'S PLAN
## I HAVE PLANS FOR YOU

*"I Have Plans for you, plans to prosper you. I will not harm you; you are my child. If you stay faithful and keep my promises, I have plans for your future." Written by Will Harris from the Songwriter's Journal Album inspired by the prophet Jeremiah*

I was born in the summer month of July in 1981 in Memphis, Tennessee. My mother named me Willie Lee Harris. I am not sure where this name comes from or why it was so prominent in her mind. I don't know of any other Willie Lees in my immediate family. As a kid, I hated my name so much that I couldn't wait until I turned eighteen. I had plans to change my name to Michael. In my mind,

Michael sounded better and not as country. Michael had a ring to it, and I felt that I would be more successful with the name Michael.

My mother's name was Alean Harris, and she was born on April 10, 1944, to the late Modell and Bertha Lee Joiner Toles. She was raised in Mississippi with eight other siblings: Lizzie, Pauline, Corrine, Robert, Richard, Bonnie, Lou, and Ozell. Mom graduated from high school in the 1960s, and like other Southern families, she migrated to Detroit, where her oldest sister Lizzie had moved. In fact, most of Mom's sisters eventually moved to Detroit in their early twenties and thirties, and they lived there for years.

While in Detroit, Mom married a man named John Harris, and that's how I got my last name. John Harris is not my father, but Mom never changed her name after their marriage. In fact, I'm not sure if they ever legally divorced. Mom's maiden name was Toles, and I always asked myself, why didn't she just give me her maiden name?

After separating from John Harris, Mom began to experience some mental issues and began seeing a psychiatrist there in Detroit. She was later diagnosed with having schizophrenia. Mom's siblings have never shared much about the experience with me, but her sister, Aunt Bonnie, who will become a very intricate part of my story, lived with Mom and witnessed Mom's behavior up close and personal and encouraged her to continue to see the psychiatrist there in Detroit.

After years of living in Detroit, Mom moved back to Mississippi as my grandfather, Modell Toles, began to distribute land to his children. She received her land, and my grandfather purchased a trailer for her to live.

## SUMMER 1981

In the summer of 1981, Mom disclosed that she was having some stomach pain and was rushed to a local hospital in Oxford, Mississippi. The doctors discovered that her blood pressure was extremely high, and in that moment, they decided that she needed to be rushed to Memphis, TN. Mom never told anyone that she was pregnant, and to this day we don't know if she knew and just felt the need to hide it, or if she just really didn't know.

Imagine a few days later, my mother, a mentally unstable woman, returning home from the hospital to the small town of Taylor, Mississippi, with a newborn baby. As I reflect on this, I can hear the conversations within the community. Did she know she was pregnant? Why didn't she tell anyone? Who's the father? Yes, this hidden secret and this newborn baby that no one knew anything about, was me. This is the beginning of my story and the beginning of the plan God had and still has for my life.

# HE KNOWS
# MY NAME

*"He Knows my pain, every struggle, He's there to comfort, He Knows my name. He'll never leave you, He'll never forsake you, a very present help in trouble, He knows my name. Written by Will Harris from the He Knows My Name Album.*

I was raised by my mother in a two-bedroom trailer in Taylor, Mississippi, for the first five years of my life. Taylor is a very small town with a population of only four hundred people. The community is a close-knit community where everybody knows everybody, and everyone is a cousin down the line somewhere.

Taylor had two stores, one for the Whites and one for the Blacks. If you were Black and didn't know everyone in the community, at some point you would meet them at the Carter's Grocery and Laundromat Store (the Carter store) or at church. Mrs. Geardie Mae Carter was the proud owner of the Carter store. I am not sure what Mrs. Carter's previous career was, but she was a math whiz. As kids, my cousins Lovell, Treion, LeAngelo, Jody, and I would go to the Carter store to buy penny candy, and we were excited to hand over our one hundred pennies. Mrs. Carter would make us stand there and count every one of those pennies out to her. She would also allow families to buy grocery items from her store for the month, and she would write what she called a ticket to be paid at the end of the month.

North Hopewell, Mt. Hope, South Hopewell, and New Jerusalem Holiness Church were the four churches in our community. We were members of North Hopewell Missionary Baptist Church, where I sat on the mourners' bench during a summer revival and prayed for salvation. In the South, feeding the Pastor Sunday dinner on Sundays after church was one of the greatest celebrations a family could host. I distinctly remember my family hosting Rev. Charles S. Pope at our home for Sunday dinner. During the dinner, he explained salvation to me and my cousins, and we were made aware that we would be seeking salvation the following week. In full transparency, this scared me more than anything I had experienced. I kept asking myself, "What happens if I don't feel the spirit like you're explaining to me? Will I have to wait until the next year to revisit the mourners' bench?" After pondering the thought of having to revisit the mourners' bench, I quickly made up my mind that I would get my religion that week and that week only.

After one intense night of pleading with God for salvation on the mourners' bench, I gave the Pastor, Rev. Charles S. Pope, my hand during his sermon on Tuesday night. I was determined not to sit on the bench for the full week of revival. I was baptized the following Sunday. I remember being so excited to receive a brand-new pair of suspenders and new dress shoes for that Sunday. I was ecstatic about receiving the new white Bible that I had seen others receive, and finally having the opportunity to receive communion. I had watched the adults take communion for years, and now I was finally able to partake. I took my salvation very seriously, and I vowed to never lose the white Bible that was given to me at baptism. To this day, I don't know what happened to that small white Bible, but it was the beginning of my relationship with God.

---

As a child, I discovered my mother's mental illness up close and personal. I can recall my mother hearing voices, and she would talk back to them. I didn't think anything of it. I thought maybe it was just normal for people to hear voices. Because of Mom's mental illness, I had very little interaction with the outside world as a kid. I do remember walking across the street to play with a neighbor, Tommy, periodically, but I was introverted and an extremely shy kid.

Around five years old, Mom's sister, Aunt Bonnie, decided to move back to Mississippi from Detroit. In her transition, she and her children moved in with me and my mother. This was exciting for me; finally, I had other people in the house that I could interact with. My Aunt Bonnie had four children, LaQuette, Veronica,

Charisse, and Lovell. I am not exactly sure how long they lived with us, but eventually, my Aunt Bonnie received her land from my grandfather, and she moved out of the house.

One cold night, my mother had a mental episode, and I remember walking the streets at what must have felt like two in the morning. I distinctly remember sitting on a swing set in my Uncle Robert's yard, and the sheriff coming to take my mother away. I didn't know where they were taking her, but I later learned that she was being admitted to a mental hospital called Whitfield. I spent that one night at my Uncle Robert's house, and then I was sent to live with Aunt Bonnie. This felt normal for me because I was very familiar with my Aunt Bonnie and her children. However, my Aunt Bonnie had married a man named Kenneth with whom I wasn't that comfortable. He was a nice man, but he wasn't sensitive to the trauma I was facing at all. Uncle Kenny made it very clear that I was just the nephew. He would make comments like, "Your Aunt Bonnie didn't have to take you in," or "She could have left you out on the streets." I was extremely shy, and it wouldn't be long before the family would become frustrated with me because I just wouldn't talk around them. I think as a kid my spirit was just broken and confused as to why my mother would be taken from me. Mom was all I knew for the first years of my life.

Eventually, I warmed up and felt good about having others around me to interact with. My Aunt Bonnie never treated me any different than her own kids. After a few years, people in the community began to think that I was actually her child, and she never made a special effort to correct them. However, she always made sure that I knew that she was my aunt, and Mom was my mom. Mom would be released periodically from the mental facility, and she would live with my grandfather only until he would get tired of her, provoke her, and then send her back. These episodes would happen frequently. The sheriff would come to pick Mom up, and it felt like everyone from the community would come outside to watch my mother be hauled back off to the mental facility. These experiences were very traumatic for me. I felt helpless, embarrassed, and confused.

As an adult reflecting on this, I just needed an adult to cover me and explain to me what was really happening. In many instances, I felt isolated and just needed to be nurtured. As a kid, I just couldn't understand why my mother had to live somewhere else hours away from me. I had an attachment to Mom that I don't think any of the family understood at the time. It had only been Mom and me for the first five years of my life. It also didn't help that my aunts and uncles did not have the language to express mental illness to a child. They would just say things like, "Your momma's just crazy, boy," or "She's on her way to Whitfield, the crazy house." I now understand that my aunts and uncles didn't use these words to hurt me, but it definitely hurt at the time.

Whitfield is a mental hospital housed on a three hundred and fifty-acre campus in Whitfield, Mississippi, just fifteen miles southeast of Jackson, Mississippi. In my mind, Whitfield was the scariest place in the world. I can remember my aunts and uncles making the drive to Jackson, Mississippi, to visit Mom at Whitfield on Saturday mornings periodically, but I was never allowed to go. I always wondered what this place was like. Sometimes I would try and allow my mind to imagine the place, but it was just too spooky for me to allow my mind to go there.

Eventually, when I was around ten or eleven, my mother came home from Whitfield, and she lived with my grandfather permanently and never returned to Whitfield. I remember being so excited as a kid when she finally came home. My grandfather lived just across the yard from where I was living with my Aunt Bonnie. Sometimes when Mom would come around, I would hear the adults in the room say, "Here comes your crazy momma, we don't feel like being bothered with her today." These words stung as a kid, and I began to resent my own family members for the words they used.

As with anyone facing a problem, my mother had difficulty acknowledging that anything was wrong with her. She refused to take her blood pressure medication, as well as the medications prescribed for her mental health. Every day, I would walk across the yard to see her, and I took pride in finally convincing her to take her medications. We would talk about school, and if I had received a solo at school, I would sing it a million times for her. She would smile and say, "Good job." She took pride in always telling me to be a good boy, and she gave me anything

I wanted. I learned responsibility at a very young age from her. At age eleven, Mom gave me my birth certificate and my Social Security card, and I guarded it with my life. She sensed that I had a level of maturity that most kids didn't have. When I would ask who my father was, she would always deflect and begin to talk about something else. I didn't know whether to attribute her evasion to mental illness or if perhaps, it was just too painful for her to discuss. After asking her for many years, I didn't want to make her uncomfortable, so I stopped asking.

# FLY HIGH

*"Fly high above any circumstance. I know you
can reach your highest potential; just believe in
your heart and hold fast to your dreams."
Dream Again Written by Will Harris from the
Dream Again Album.*

O ne afternoon in high school, I was
called to the office and told that I was
leaving school. When I arrived at the
office, it was my Aunt Lou who had come to
pick me up. Aunt Lou shared with me that
Mom had a stroke and had to be rushed to the
hospital. When we arrived, Mom was inco-
herent and hooked up to a lot of machines.
After Mom's stroke, she never fully regained

mobility on her right side and had to be placed in a nursing home.

Visiting Mom at the nursing home was difficult for me. It was devastating that Mom would be in the nursing home at such a young age. Each time I visited, she seemed so depressed and unhappy. Mom was only fifty years old when she had the stroke, and eventually, her father, my grandfather, would live right down the hall from her at Graceland Nursing Home Facility in Oxford. I had become frustrated with God at this point. It seemed that my peers' parents were young, vibrant, and very active in their lives, and it bothered me that I just didn't have the normal life they had. In fact, I became depressed each time I went to see her. I just hated to see her in a nursing home facility. Each time I visited Mom, she would always talk to me about being a good boy and beamed with joy each time she had an opportunity to introduce me as her son to one of the nurses who would periodically stop by the room. Mom instilled in me respect and love for everyone. After each visit, she would always say, "Be respectful and a good boy now."

I also learned respect at a young age from community leaders. I particularly learned discipline and respect from my bus driver, Mr. Hugh Ivy, better known as "Bitter." Every morning, we would rush out to the bus stop around 6:45 a.m. because we knew if Bitter didn't see us standing at the bus stop waiting for him, he would go off and leave us. Rain, snow, sleet, or shine, you had better be standing there at the bus stop. I'm not sure where his nickname Bitter came from, but as kids, everyone on the bus called him Bitter. After years of being called Bitter, he stopped the bus one day and demanded that we start calling him Mr. Ivy. Mr. Ivy was very strict. We had assigned seats on the bus, and chewing gum and eating candy were strictly forbidden. At the beginning of each school year, he would give us a long lecture about his rules, and we developed a great deal of respect for him. I always admired the way he took a real interest in disciplining us.

In middle school, I began to come out of my shell a little and decided to run for Student Council, where I remained throughout high school. I also found the confidence to run for Most Talented and Most Likely to Succeed, and I won every year. However, my greatest joy was The Lafayette High School MS-932nd ROTC Program run by Lt. Colonel Dennis

Ramsey. Colonel Ramsey was a very intelligent, retired Air Force Lt. Colonel. God set it up perfectly. Colonel Ramsey was the perfect man to bring me out of my shell. During the first week of the program, we were told to get into formation, and Colonel Ramsey called me out and asked me to sing the National Anthem on the spot. From that moment, I began to soar in the ROTC Program, and my leadership skills were being developed.

During my sophomore year, I was asked to direct the school's ROTC Choir after its founder, Marcus Harden, had graduated. I was excited because this would be my first real experience at training a large choir. The ROTC Choir became popular, and before I knew it, we were giving concerts and performances at many churches and nursing homes, including Graceland where Mom was. It was a joy to perform with the choir where Mom lived, but also a bit uncomfortable. I had anxiety about my peers seeing my mother in a wheelchair and living in a nursing home.

Mrs. Peggy Tubbs, my high school chorus teacher, noticed that I had a unique gift for music. She would allow me to warm the choir up on some days, and for one spring concert, she asked that I teach the choir two gospel songs. I was so excited to be able to teach gospel music to the chorus. I taught "Perfect Praise" by Walt Whitman and "Gotta Feeling" by O'landa Draper. I was fascinated with the music of O'landa Draper because he was from Memphis, and his choir was very charismatic. Mrs. Tubbs took a special interest in me. I'm sure she was aware of my family dynamics, and she went above and beyond what a normal chorus teacher would do. She would register me for solo performances each year, and she would drive me to Tupelo, Mississippi, to compete in vocal competitions.

One year, I entered the Mid-South Faith Youth Talent Competition, and I also entered the ROTC choir that I directed. I selected the song "Angels Among Us" by a group called Alabama for myself, and I taught the choir "What if God Is Unhappy with Our Praise." I won first place, and the choir won the overall grand prize. I remember being so happy that I had won, but no one was there to celebrate with me. I ran to the payphone to call my Aunt Bonnie to let her know that I had won and that I needed a ride home. We only had one car in the household, which made participating in any extracurricular activities nearly impossible. For the most part, I stayed away from activities that required me to stay after school because I knew it would be difficult getting a ride home. My Uncle Kenny was the only one who drove, and he had no real interest in my life or what I was doing. I always wondered how it would be to have a real dad who supported my dreams and goals and took a real interest in me. By the time I was a teenager, I had become numb to the pain of not having a father, and anytime anyone would ask me about it, I was quick to shut them down with a firm "it doesn't bother me."

My Uncle Kenny worked for the University of Mississippi Golf Course, and on Saturday mornings, my cousin Lovell and I would wake up early, excited to go to work with him. Lovell and I were two peas in a pod. Two sisters' children born in the same month and the same year. Lovell was born on July 9, and I was born on July 21. We were more like brothers growing up. My Uncle Kenny always showed more interest in Lovell. Though my aunt made me feel like I was actually her son, my uncle made it very clear that I was just the nephew. When we would go to work with him, he would only let Lovell drive the golf carts while we were on the golf course. In our teenage years, he taught Lovell how to drive, but he wouldn't teach me. Uncle Kenny had a love for working on cars. He would always call Lovell outside to help hold the flashlight or to hand him tools to work on the car, but he would never ask me. He seemed to take interest in my musical abilities, but other than music, we didn't talk about much. One night after a revival service, he yelled, "Boy, you need to learn how to play in some other keys." This was embarrassing but it pushed me to learn how to play in all keys. I tried hard for music to be my gateway with him, but I quickly realized that music wasn't going to be enough to win him over. I began to realize that he would never be able to give me the love and affection I yearned for from my father.

# My Father/The Mystery

After Mom's passing, I was confused, hurt, and bitter with God. There were so many unanswered questions. One of the biggest issues I had with God was that I didn't have an opportunity to get answers from Mom about who my father was. I had heard most of my life that during my conception, she had been spending time with a man named Alonzo Paten, who they believed to be my father. Years later, through a Census Report, I learned that he was referred to as Lonzo, and his birth name was Elonzo.

Mr. Paten never made an effort to meet me, and no one in my family ever tried to reach out to him on my behalf. Periodically, my Aunt

Bonnie would ask me if it bothered me, and I would lie and pretend that I didn't care. In my early years, I really didn't care, but as I grew older, I just wanted to belong and be claimed as some man's son. In retrospect, Mom was very private and mentally unstable. This explains why none of her siblings even knew that she was pregnant with me.

Three years after Mom died, Mr. Paten passed away. His family contacted my family and asked if I would attend the service. I attended the service and met his other children. Surprisingly, some of them were singers, and they sang and played at his funeral service. My friends Xavier and Vincent from Rust College, and my friend Jeffrey attended the service with me. As the family began to line up, I heard the funeral director begin to line everyone up according to relation. It felt strange being placed in the lineup as a son of a man whom I had never met. As I walked down the aisle of the small funeral home chapel to view my father's body, I had a million things running through my mind. What are people thinking? Are his other children wondering who I am? Will I look like him? When I reached the casket, I took a deep breath and relaxed a little. He was a brown-skinned older gentleman, and I couldn't really tell if I had any of his features. Besides, I am my mom's twin, and I have more of her features.

The funeral service was beautiful, and I had an opportunity to hear his daughters sing and lead the music. When the service was over, I was invited to take pictures with his other children, but we didn't exchange any contact information. I told myself that I was ending this chapter and would never contact them again. At the time, I felt strong about not wanting to disrupt their lives with the questions I had about my father, and I did not contact them again until years later.

In 2019, in the height of the COVID-19 pandemic, I decided to take a step towards learning more about my father. During this time, the church closed, and I wasn't rehearsing nearly as much. My days were spent writing music and reflecting a lot. I felt an overwhelming desire to begin the search to discover who my father was, and I wanted to find out who I truly was. In my research, I discovered through a census that my father was born in 1930 and was raised in Lafayette Springs, a small rural town outside of Oxford, Mississippi. I also discovered that he was a carpenter and a plumber until his mental health began to fail him, and he was no longer able to work. This information was a bit frightening, but it helped me to put some of the pieces of the puzzle together. I also learned that he had also spent many years as a patient at the mental facility Whitfield.

The journey began with a phone call to Hodges Funeral Home in my hometown of Oxford, Mississippi. I contacted Hodges to get information on my father. I remember my father's funeral being held at Hodges, and I was sure the funeral home would still have his obituary. After speaking with the funeral home, I learned that they had gone through a fire, and many of the files were destroyed. Ms. LaVera Hodges, who ran the funeral home, stated that she knew my relatives. This was a little difficult for me, but I trusted LaVera. LaVera was one of the choir directors at Second Baptist Church when I played there, and I had total trust and faith in her. LaVera suggested that I begin searching for my father's oldest daughter, Alberta, on social media.

I stood in my kitchen, making a cup of coffee, struggling to type an appropriate message. I grappled with what to say. *Will she remember me from the funeral service? Will she think I'm some deranged person?* Finally, I found the words and sent the message. Within ten minutes, Alberta responded, "Yes, I know who you are. You are my brother." My heart dropped, and we began to communicate. We arranged a time to converse over the phone the following Saturday, and Alberta welcomed me to the family. Her tone was so welcoming and warm; I felt very comfortable talking with her. She explained that our dad had spent some time in a mental institution. She expressed that he might have met my mom at a mental health appointment. She shared stories of Dad with me that really helped me to put the pieces of the puzzle together. I realized she was essentially describing me.

Later, I was introduced to a cousin named Joanne, who stated that Dad was her favorite uncle. Joanne provided me with more insight, and then I realized that she had preached Dad's eulogy. For weeks, I wrestled with whether I wanted to move forward with truly discovering if Lonzo was my father. On most days, I was fine with never knowing the truth, and on other days, I felt that I just needed to know.

After speaking with a mentor about some things happening in my life, she raised the question, "Have you ever just sat with yourself and asked the question, who am I?" This question turned the green light on for me. For most of my life, I felt like I was in this world all alone. Both parents deceased and no biological siblings. I had no real reference for who I was. This simple question gave me the confidence to begin the journey of discovering who I really am.

In 2024, I found the courage to ask my sister Alberta to do a sibling DNA test with me. She was thrilled and more than happy to comply. On a Tuesday morning, I walked into a DNA testing center to complete the test. My mind was all over the place, and my heart was racing. The nurse who administered the test wanted to chat, and I wasn't in the mood to talk to anyone. She began to ask questions, and I shared with her that I was writing a book, and this was one of the missing pieces. The test was scheduled to begin at 9:30 a.m., but she didn't arrive until 9:45 a.m. She was excited to hear that I was writing a book and gave me permission to write about her, but she requested that I not mention her tardiness. Sadly, I don't remember her name, but she was the angel sent by God to calm my nerves and help me through the test.

Two days later, Alberta went to a testing site in her hometown of Poplar Bluff, Missouri, to complete her test. One week later, the results were sent to me on a Friday evening. I had just finished teaching piano students for the evening and was on my way to have a quiet dinner alone when I saw the email come through. I sat in my car in the parking lot of Bonefish Grill and quietly read the results. The DNA results revealed that the probability of half-siblingship between Alberta and me was 99.9 percent. Lonzo Paten was indeed my father.

# MY EARLY MUSIC LIFE

*"We Don't get in the spirit like we used to, We don't get in the spirit like we used to, that's what's wrong with the church today we let the devil steal our praise, and we don't get in the spirit like we used to"*

I received my first solo in church at around age seven. I practiced, practiced, and practiced the song "We Don't Get in the Spirit Like We Used To." The hardest part for me was learning to adlib and create lyrics that actually made sense. I thought I had done a decent job, but after the worship service, one of the members complained that I was too young to be singing a song with those lyrics. My spirit was crushed, and I never really wanted to sing a solo in church again.

Around the age of six or seven, my love for gospel music began. My Aunt Bonnie's daughter, Veronica, is seven years older than me, and she loved gospel music. She is the real singer in our entire family. Veronica would visit Sound Shop, a music store in Oxford, and purchase cassette tapes and eventually CDs of BeBe and CeCe, The Clark Sisters, Commissioned, Helen Baylor, The New Jersey Mass Choir, Milton Brunson, and others. Because they had moved from Detroit, we listened to all the great gospel artists from the city of Detroit.

One day, my aunt discovered that I was playing the piano on the coffee table, and she said, "I think he might be a musician." I remember getting my first keyboard for Christmas that year and playing it all night. I taught myself every scale. My love for music became so intense that while most kids were outside playing basketball and football, I would be outside playing the piano on the back of someone's car or standing and directing the choir in midair. When I was left at home alone, I would blast the CD player and direct the choir in the mirror. I'm sure the other kids thought I was crazy, but I didn't care. I began listening to the music and dissecting the harmonies and realized that I had a pretty decent singing voice.

Eventually, we started a family gospel singing group called the Gospel Four, and we would travel and sing. Veronica was our primary soloist, but I would lead a few songs with the group. As a kid, I had a natural falsetto voice, and I would walk around the house always picking out the soprano and alto part of any song. My cousin Lovell would always tease me about it. Today, I am naturally a baritone, but I have a very strong falsetto voice, which has helped me clearly teach soprano and alto parts to choirs with ease.

As a child, I was a part of the BICY Youth Community Choir under the direction of James Brassell. James had a passion for youth in our community and brought together youth singers from Abbeville, Taylor, Water Valley, Flint Hill, and other places. James would secure the van from Harrisonville Missionary Baptist Church and drive for hours to pick us all up, and after rehearsals, he would drive from community to community to get us back home.

I also had the opportunity to join the Voices of North Mississippi Community Choir when I was fourteen years old. The Voices of North Mississippi were under the direction of Herbert Bonner, and his baby brother Cassie Bonner would assist him periodically. Herbert was a masterful organist and had a phenomenal ear for teaching voice parts. Veronica was initially a member of this choir, and I would go to rehearsal with her and stand on the wall desperately waiting for someone to let me sing. One day, Herbert invited me to join, and I was the happiest kid in the world. These choir experiences developed my love and respect for gospel music. The Voices of North Mississippi would rehearse on Sundays at the Best Western Hotel in Oxford, and seasoned singers from all over North Mississippi would come to sing. At each performance, just before we would sing, Herbert would signal for us to go out to get robed up and in formation. On most concerts, we were the special guests, and we would process down the aisle wearing our gold and green robes. The choir had a clean signature sound that was distinct, and I took pride in being the youngest member. Each week, I couldn't wait for Sundays to rehearse with Herbert and the

Voices. This all came to a screeching halt when my sister Veronica decided that she no longer wanted to sing with the choir. Transportation to and from rehearsals became difficult for me, and I eventually had to leave the choir.

---

When I was thirteen years old, I received my first church job as the musician for Jordan Chapel CME Church. This didn't last long because I wasn't used to being in church every Sunday, so I quit. During those days, most churches met twice a month, and I was accustomed to being at home enjoying my Sundays off.

One evening, a lady showed up at our home and asked my Aunt Bonnie if she could hire me to play the piano for her family's choir. Mrs. Vermacy Tyson Smith was the wife of Rev. Christopher Smith, who was the Pastor of Greater New Hope Baptist Church in Myrtle, Mississippi. My Aunt approved, and before I knew it, I was playing the piano and directing a family choir by the name of the Gospel Friends. In preparation for their upcoming concert, I taught and arranged most of their music.

This family choir became my second family. The Tysons would pick me up on the back of their truck and drive me to rehearsal. I would spend some nights with them and travel all over, singing and playing for them. It didn't hurt that my girlfriend, Anitra, was a member of this family, and this meant that I would get to spend more time with her. It wasn't long before Vermacy's husband asked me to become his Minister of Music at Greater New Hope Baptist Church in Myrtle, Mississippi.

These years were solid musical training years for me. Greater New Hope paid me forty-five dollars a week to play and lead their music ministry. I had the full responsibility of training the choir, playing, and planning concerts. I took this role seriously. I would type the lyrics to songs for the choir while at school and ask my teachers for permission to make copies for my choir rehearsals. After a few years of leading the music ministry at Greater New Hope, my Aunt Bonnie demanded that I come back to my home church, Jeffries Chapel, and become the musician. She always said that I could play where I wanted when I turned eighteen, but home would always come first. Both churches were only having worship twice a month, and I would attend Jeffries Chapel on the first and third Sundays, and then I would lead the music ministry at Greater New Hope on the second and fourth Sundays. This was a difficult transition for me because Jeffries Chapel didn't want me as the Minister of Music; they only wanted a musician. Greater New Hope gave me the confidence in training choirs, teaching parts, and directing. At Jeffries Chapel, I was just a musician.

While at Jeffries Chapel, I met Michael Gordon, who is now Pastor Michael Gordon. Michael was three years older than me with a very soulful, southern voice. Michael invited me to join a singing quartet group called God's Gift. In my hometown, quartet music was very prominent and "the thing to do." After a few years of being with the quartet group, they began to feel like a family. We would travel every weekend, and we began to build lasting relationships with other groups who would be on the program with us. Singing gospel quartet music certainly gave me the confidence in my musical ad-libbing abilities, but it was never my first love. I always loved choir music. I knew in my heart that I was a choir boy, and quartet music wasn't it for me.

# LEARNING THE PIANO

My mother and I received a disability check due to her mental illness. My check was two hundred fifty dollars per month, but my grandfather would only give my Aunt Bonnie forty dollars a month from the check to help support me. My Aunt decided that she would use the money to pay for my piano lessons. I always thought that maybe my grandfather was saving this money for a college fund for me, but sadly after his death, I discovered that he had not saved it for me.

I met my first piano teacher when I was in the third grade at Lafayette Elementary School. Lafayette had a general music program and a gifted music program. Mrs. Gaye Calhoun was a very gifted, innovative music teacher with black hair and eyes that would pierce your soul. One day, Mrs. Calhoun came to talk to our class about the gifted music program, and I was selected. At the time, I didn't know how I got into the program, but later in life, Mrs. Calhoun revealed that initially, she wasn't going to accept me. She felt I was too shy and timid. Mrs. Eulastine Thompson, an African American third-grade teacher from my hometown, explained to Mrs. Calhoun my story and convinced her to let me in the program.

Eventually, I began to take formal piano lessons from Mrs. Calhoun, and I loved it. Unfortunately, my musical background was strictly church, and learning to read music wasn't on my radar. I wanted to play for a black church, and in my hometown, all of the musicians played by ear. I felt that learning Beethoven wasn't going to help me become the musician I wanted to be, so I stopped taking lessons. This was a terrible mistake. I learned it was a mistake when I entered college and decided that I would become a music major.

My Aunt Bonnie was a very spiritual woman. We were members of a Baptist church, but at home, we were more Bapti-Costal (my version of Baptist and Pentecostal). Family prayer was a must in our household, and nothing was shocking about being awakened in the middle of the night to my Aunt Bonnie praying and speaking in tongues. My Aunt Bonnie developed friendships with a lot of evangelists who traveled and led revivals. I can remember for a while it felt as if we were traveling every night of the week to go to church somewhere. All the holiness churches would stay in church for hours, and I would say to myself, "Does it take all of this?" It didn't matter where we went, the evangelist would always call me up to the front to prophesy to me. During this time, I was extremely shy, and my heart would hit the floor every time it would happen. It began to happen so often that I began not wanting to go to church anymore.

One afternoon, we were visiting New Jerusalem Pentecostal Holiness Church, and Pastor Ora Lee Egerson called me to the front. I was saying to myself, "Oh no, not again." At this point, I was over it and didn't want another preacher calling me up front. She told me to lift my hands and spoke over my life. She told me that I would be a great musician someday, and then she told me to go and play something on the piano. I was sweating bullets. I was saying to myself, "Is she serious? The only thing I know is Beethoven, and this isn't going to work in this holiness church." I wasn't even playing full chords at that time; I was only playing with two fingers. I slowly moved to the piano, and I used those two fingers and began playing shouting and dancing music. They danced in the spirit for quite a while. This was the defining moment of my life where I began to accept that my calling would be in Music Ministry.

# RESILIENCE
## THE CAPACITY TO WITHSTAND OR TO RECOVER QUICKLY FROM DIFFICULTIES.

I excelled in ROTC, and during my senior year, I was selected and given the highest rank of Cadet Colonel and named the Corps Commander for the entire ROTC Program. The ceremony was held in our school's common area on a cold, fall day. Aunt Bonnie, Aunt Lou, and my mother attended. I took great pride in this honor, and I was so grateful that Mom could attend. My role as the Corps Commander stretched me in many ways and forced me out of my introverted comfort zone.

After high school, I attended Northwest Community College in Senatobia, Mississippi. In my hometown, this was the college that most students would attend. We would always joke and say that we were all going to the thirteenth grade at Northwest because that's where everyone went to school. To be honest, I wasn't educated on other schools and opportunities I could have taken advantage of, nor was I aware of the amazing musical opportunities. A full-time career in music was unheard of, and I had no real blueprint to follow. I thought of a career in the military, but my Aunt Bonnie didn't think it was a wise decision. The only thing she could think about was me being sent to war, and that scared both me and her.

During the summer after graduation, I worked hard, playing the piano on Sunday mornings, teaching piano lessons, and playing for weddings. I saved up five hundred dollars as a down payment for my first car and purchased a Navy Blue 1986 Oldsmobile Cutlass Ciera.

On a hot summer morning in August, I packed my Oldsmobile and drove up Interstate 55 North to Senatobia, Mississippi, to move into the dorm at Northwest Community College. When I arrived, I observed parents there to help students move into the dorm room. I couldn't help but feel sad that I had no one there to help me celebrate this accomplishment, nor was there anyone there to help me move and get settled into my dorm room. This was the first time I realized that the stakes were high, and that I had no choice but to get an education. I was determined to be successful.

During my freshman year, I gained the courage to become a music major and studied voice with Mrs. Suzanne VanDyke. As a music major at Northwest, I learned for the first time that I was actually a Baritone and not a Tenor. I sang Bass in the choir and enjoyed studying Italian Arias. It was my first time studying classical vocal music. Mrs. VanDyke encouraged me to audition for a show that the theater was sponsoring, and I was asked to play the leading role as Homer in *Lilies of the Field* based on the 1963 movie starring Sidney Poitier. This was my first acting role, and being cast as the lead role was a bit overwhelming. The show ran for almost two months, and at the end of each show, I received a standing ovation. The show was a perfect way to end my freshman year at Northwest, and I was looking forward to enjoying the summer break.

# GALLERY

*My Mother Alean Toles Harris*

*Will and Aunt Bonnie*

*Mom, Aunt Bonnie and Will*

*The Gospel Four Family Singing Group*
*Veronica, Charisse, Will and Lovell*

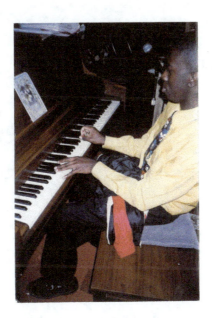

*Will playing the piano at Pleasant Green*
*Church*

*Will directing the ROTC Choir during a
Spring Concert*

*Will directing the ROTC Choir at
Graceland Nursing Home*

*Will competing in the 1999 Mid South Fair*
*Youth Competition*

*Will Graduation from Rust College*

*Will's Recording Choir Will Harris and
Friends 10 Year Music Celebration*

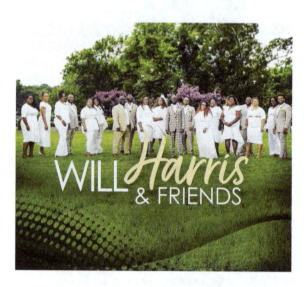

*Will's Recording Choir Will Harris and
Friends from the Heal Our Land Project*

# MOM'S DECLINE

## GOD WILL TAKE CARE OF YOU

*"Broken Hearted, Feeling Lonely, God will,*
*Surely He will, God will Take Care of You"*
*Lyrics from Will Harris's arrangement of*
*God will Take Care of You*
*from the Songwriter's Journal Album*

During the summer after my freshman year of college, I was hired as the pianist at Second Baptist Church in Oxford, MS. As a child, Second Baptist was the "It" Church. Their pastor was Rev. Dr. Leroy Wadlington, a very successful and educated theologian. Second Baptist had a reputation for being bougie, but I loved that they wore choir robes and seemed to be so professional. This was the dream job for me. The music ministry at Second Baptist was led by Pastor Wadling-ton's son, Lemont Wadlington. Lemont was an awesome musician who was a very gifted organ-ist. Periodically, he would ask me to teach or direct the choir.

While at Second Baptist, my mother's health began to decline. I received a phone call that Mom had been rushed to the hospital from the nursing home. I went to the hospital to visit Mom, and she wasn't coherent. Her kidneys and liver had begun to fail, and I knew that it wouldn't be long before she would be gone. On a beautiful Saturday evening, June 28, 2002, Mom passed away.

We held Mom's funeral service one week later on Saturday, July 6, 2002. This would be the first time I had ever entered a funeral home to make funeral plans. My aunts and uncles sat with me as we picked out her casket and her dress. I selected a pink casket and a beautiful light pink dress for her. On the evening before her service, we were instructed to come back to the funeral home to view her body and give approval. I waited most of the day to hear from my family, only to find out that they had al-ready gone. I forced myself to go alone and view her body. I drove around the funeral home for at least an hour trying to convince myself to go in. I remember walking into Hodges Funeral Home to view her body. The owner, Mrs. Lavera Hodges, walked me into the room and stood with me. I cried, prayed, and released her. Mom had a beautiful funeral service, and she is buried in the Yocona Cemetery at our home church, North Hopewell Missionary Baptist Church in Taylor, MS.

# RUST COLLEGE

While attending Northwest Community College in Senatobia, MS, I received a phone call from a friend saying that Rust College in Holly Springs, MS, was looking for a musician for their BSU gospel choir. Rust College is a small, historically black, liberal arts college founded in 1866, located approximately thirty-five miles southeast of Memphis, TN. I was familiar with Rust because my cousin Veronica had graduated from Rust, and as a child, I would watch their renowned A'Cappella Choir on TV on Sunday mornings.

The Rust College Gospel Choir also had a reputation for excellence, and my cousin Veronica

would come home from college on the week-
ends and share stories about their gospel choir.
One year, I had the opportunity to attend the
live recording titled *Dr. Mattie Moss Clark
presents Corey Skinner's Collegiate Voices of
Faith*. This was the Baptist Student Union
Gospel Choir of Rust College, but the name
was changed for the recording. The choir was
known for their dynamic previous director,
Mr. James O. Pope of Memphis, TN, and
other phenomenal directors. James was an
amazing organist and the grandson of Rev. C.
S. Pope, my childhood pastor. Today, he has
become a very good friend and colleague.

I began driving to Rust once a week from Senatobia to rehearse with the gospel choir, and
after a while, I had taken over and become their
official director. The Gospel Choir was considered extracurricular, and the school gave us no
support at all. We would travel and win competitions each year, but Rust College refused to
support the gospel choir. The choir was advised by Masheeta Lindsey Hill, who was a no-
nonsense person. She loved the choir and
would go to war with anyone in administration
for her BSU Students. She worked hard each
year encouraging us to keep striving, even

though the administration gave us no support. We worked hard throughout the year sponsoring fundraisers and putting nickels and dimes together to rent buses, so that we could travel and sing at local churches. The school had a bus and several vans, but we were not allowed to use the school's transportation. Most evening classes at Rust ended at 9:00 p.m., and the Gospel Choir would rehearse at 10:00 p.m. on Wednesday nights in the Doxey Auditorium on campus.

After completing two years at Northwest, I resigned as the choir director at Rust and transferred to Mississippi College, where I studied music with Dr. Ed Dacchuss. Mississippi College was a Southern Baptist School located in the heart of Clinton, just outside of Jackson, Mississippi.

Again, I loaded my car and drove the three hours to Jackson alone and moved into the dorm at Mississippi College, affectionately known as MC. MC had a great spiritual environment, and we had chapel twice a week. MC was proving to be a great experience, but I just couldn't seem to focus. Mom's passing had my mind all over the place, and living in a big city like Jackson was so different from what I was used to. While in Jackson, I played for Terry Grove Baptist Church and enjoyed working with their choirs. After a year at MC, I decided that Jackson wasn't for me, and that I was moving to Memphis, TN. I moved to Memphis and now found myself enrolled as an official student at Rust College. I was already familiar with many of the students and faculty because of my affiliation with the Gospel Choir. I lived in Memphis, TN, and commuted thirty to forty-five minutes to Rust College every day.

The gospel choir was branched under the Baptist Student Union, and we affectionately called it the BSU Choir. We worked all year long for the State and National Baptist Student Union Retreat. During the retreat, we attended spiritual seminars, but the highlight of the retreat was the choir competition. Our state retreat was always held in Jackson, Mississippi, and we would compete against some of the finest gospel choirs in the state, including Mississippi Valley State University, Hinds Community College, and other choirs. On the National level, we would attend the National Baptist Student Union Retreat and compete against Fort Valley State University, Prairie View A &

M University, Lamar University, East Tennessee State University, and other choirs. During these days, I began developing my songwriting abilities by arranging medleys for the choir. I took pride in creating themes each year for the choir to present during competition. Each year at the retreat, my friend, Hammond Organist James O. Pope Jr., would fill the hotel's ballroom with the sound of the Hammond Organ, and he would play "Amazing Grace" and "Lift Every Voice and Sing." Conductor, the late Dr. Anthony B. Stinson, would conduct and lead the choir in a very admirable and distinguished way. I was so in awe that I began patterning myself after Dr. Stinson.

Directing the gospel choir at Rust was truly the opportunity I needed to stretch me as a musician and a songwriter. Training the singers at Rust allowed me to develop my own style and sound. The diction and the vocal color of the voices you hear in my choirs today began with the gospel choir at Rust College. Most years, we would walk away with the first-place trophy from our choir competitions. I took pride in creating a distinct yet mature sound for the choir. I trained them to sing with just enough vibrato to bring color to the notes but strived to never let the vibrato distort the sound or the clarity of the words. Most of the other college choirs were directed by professors or faculty members from the college. I believe we were able to stand out to the judges because I was a young student director with an unusual level of skill and creativity for my age. Each year, we would receive wonderful critiques and feedback from the judges, which helped to develop the musician I am today.

# ZEBEDEE JONES, MY MUSIC MENTOR

While at Rust, I studied as a music major with Mr. Zebedee Reynolds Jones. Though Mr. Jones was on the faculty as a voice professor, most of his attention was focused on his beloved A'Capella Choir. Arriving at choir rehearsal even one minute late was unacceptable to Mr. Jones. The A'Capella Choir at Rust was the school's official choir and received funding from the school. The tension between the gospel choir and the concert choir had grown so great that Mr. Jones decided music majors would no longer be able to participate in both choirs. However, he made an exception for me because I was the director of the gospel choir.

Mr. Jones was a strict choir director who tolerated no nonsense from anyone. I was always fascinated with his style because he drove a beautiful white Lincoln with a navy-blue top. His license plate read "Acapella," in honor of the A'Capella Choir. Mr. Jones was also the Minister of Music at Centenary United Methodist Church in Memphis. He would often share his experiences with me as a Minister of Music, and I couldn't wait until I was able to secure a full-time Minister of Music job. Mr. Jones was a perfectionist with his music. Most singers in the choir at Rust were non-music majors and did not read music well. Mr. Jones would sit at the piano and play each part over and over again. The choir was only scheduled to meet on Mondays, Wednesdays, and Fridays, but he would make us rehearse every day.

When we had a big performance, he would call sectionals during lunch. Figuring out how to eat lunch after he called a rehearsal during your lunch period was the easy part. The difficult part was getting through one of his sectionals. Often, he would announce at the end of rehearsal, "On tomorrow you will need to know all verses to 'I'll Meet You in the Morning.'" This was the choir's signature song, and we performed it at every concert. He would make you stand up one by one and recite the words, and if you missed one line in any verse, he would yell, "Get Out!" Each week, the choir would start with forty to fifty members, and by the end of each week, he would get mad and put everybody out of the choir. You could not be late, and he dared you to miss a rehearsal.

As a music major, he would send me to the practice room to practice classical music, and I would always find my mind drifting to something gospel. One day, he banged on the practice room door and told me he didn't want to hear any gospel and to get back to playing what he had instructed. During those years, I began to regret not continuing my formal piano lessons. I had a magnificent ear for music, and if I heard the music just once, I could play it by ear. Mr. Jones wasn't having it. He forced me to sit with the music and learn to read. Today, I am grateful for his push.

The A'Capella Choir had an extensive traveling schedule, and we were gone every weekend during the school year. Each Christmas, the choir would present an extravagant Christmas concert in the Doxey Auditorium. We would sing music from Handel's *Messiah*, and one of my favorites was a Christmas Spiritual titled, "Round De Glory Manger."

I struggled being a Minister of Music while in college because of the choir's schedule. Mr. Jones always made an exception for me until one day I was late for a graduation performance. I was playing for Lewis Street Baptist Church in Memphis, TN, and graduation at Rust was always held on a Sunday. After church, I sped down Highway 78 to get to the graduation performance. I rushed into the gymnasium, and the choir was just getting ready to perform. I put my choir robe on and ran over to the bleachers to sit with the choir. Mr. Jones stood the choir to sing, and after the song, he whispered to one of the choir members, "Tell him to take my robe off, turn it in, and get out." I took the robe off and walked out of the gymnasium just as fast as I had walked in. I was so embarrassed.

Mr. Jones had a natural ability to intertwine his own story into the music while he was teaching. He possessed a southern humor while teaching and would tell us stories about growing up in Rosedale, Mississippi. He would often compare our bad singing to an imaginary place called "Plumnelly." When he used the word Plumnelly, you knew your singing was terrible. When he heard a bad note, he would bang on the piano and say, "I don't want to hear any Plumnelly singing." I use this expression with my choirs today. He demanded that you smile the entire time you sang. In the early days, women couldn't wear certain hairstyles, and he would jokingly say to the women, "Get somebody to curl your hair, gal, and put you some makeup on." He was a stickler for presentation, and the music had to be done well.

After my second year at Rust, Mr. Jones named me the Student Director for the A'Capella Choir. In this new role, I was his shadow. I had to know what key every song was in, and I had to be prepared to conduct any song he taught. Mr. Jones instilled in me the confidence I needed to lead a choir. At the end of each school year, the choir would do a two-week tour. We would begin our tour in St. Louis, MO, and then travel to Iowa, Chicago, Milwaukee, Minnesota, and Detroit. We would stay in the homes of alumni members of the college. Spending time with the alumni gave me a sense of hope. Many of them lived in beautiful homes and had great careers, and they loved to share their experiences of being students at Rust.

My Senior Recital at Rust was held on a Thursday night, and I sang music from Handel's *Messiah*, Gershwin's *Porgy and Bess*, and my final song was a spiritual titled "Sweet Jesus" by Wendell Whalum. Mr. Jones sat on the front row with tears flowing from his eyes. He yelled from the audience, "You better sing it, boy, I mean you better

sing it."

Three days after I began writing this chapter, Mr. Jones passed away at his home in Rosedale, Mississippi. I was in shock because I had plans of calling him to reveal that I was writing a chapter about him. In 2022, I made a post on Facebook about him, and I expressed that I would not be the musician I am today if it were not for him. I am thankful that I had an opportunity to honor him while he was alive. His legacy will forever live on through myself and the countless lives of many Rust College students whom he touched through music.

# Perseverance

## The Lifter

*"Persistence in doing something despite difficulty or delay in achieving success."*

While at Rust, I struggled to focus and faced financial difficulties. I worked as a security guard and served two churches, Antioch Baptist Church as the Minister of Music, and Golden Gate Cathedral Full Gospel Baptist Church as a pianist. Both churches were led by dynamic leaders, Pastor Carl Shields and Bishop Ed Stephens.

At Antioch Baptist, Pastor Shields allowed me to soar as a Minister of Music. I took pride in presenting theme-filled concerts, which were unusual for Memphis. One year, we presented an evening of hymns and spirituals, with the choir wearing gowns and tuxedos. The congregation was in awe of our presentation.

While at Golden Gate, I had the opportunity to work with one of Memphis' finest, Minister Billy Rivers. In fact, I did my internship as a music major at Golden Gate with Billy. Billy was instrumental in showing me the administrative side of leading a music ministry. He was well-organized and prepared music for the ministry a month in advance. He always led praise and worship with one upbeat song and one slow worship song. Billy was a stickler for excellence and demanded it from his musicians. There were nights when the musicians would rehearse until midnight. He would rehearse the choir, and if anyone stood up to leave, he would stop the rehearsal and ask, "Where are you going?" I was amazed that he would question adults about their departure, but the members of Golden Gate's Choir had great respect for him. Golden Gate was a magnet for great music because many choir members also sang in Billy's auditioned choir, The Angelic Voices of Faith, which was Memphis' premiere choir.

I graduated with a bachelor's degree in music from Rust on a beautiful Sunday afternoon in April. Graduation Day began with a breakfast for students and parents and was filled with events throughout the day. My Aunt Bonnie, Aunt Lou, and Uncle Kenny attended. I have only one picture from that day because my Uncle Kenny complained about the day being too long and his eagerness to leave. Despite the limited family attendance and my uncle's haste to leave, I was excited to have achieved this milestone. I knew my mother would have been proud and smiling down on me.

After graduation, I auditioned for a full-time Minister of Music job in Panama City, Florida. The church offered me the job, but I declined. A few months later, I responded to an ad for a Minister of Music job in Fayetteville, NC. Sitting at my desk in my one-bedroom apartment in Memphis, I prayed for God to open a door for me. My dream was to be a high school chorus teacher, but I was open to whatever God had planned for me.

Interviewing at Lewis Chapel felt like interviewing at the White House. Dr. John D. Fuller, Sr., had been the pastor there for forty years. He was a tall, brown-skinned, no-nonsense man. The interview weekend began on a Friday evening, allowing me to meet the music staff, who seemed very supportive. I learned that out of hundreds of applicants, four were selected to audition.

On Saturday, I was given thirty minutes with each of their choirs and an hour with their youth choir, who would be performing the next day. Members of their music selection committee scored me as I taught the choirs.

On Sunday, I led worship for two services and underwent a formal interview. I've never been one to sell myself well; I've always been someone who simply gets the job done. Of the many questions asked by the eighteen-person interview panel, one stands out. A former educator in the room said, "I've been in the choir for many, many years, and I am a wonderful soloist. No one knows that I can sing as well as I do. Discover me." Unsure of how I answered her scenario question, I later learned that I did not get the job. Today, I joke that this question might be the reason why I didn't secure the position.

During the summer after graduation, I searched and prayed to God to help me find a music teaching job, and He answered my prayers three days before the school year began. The Collegiate School of Memphis hired me as their General Music and Chorus Teacher. Collegiate was a private Christian school nestled in the heart of Memphis, TN. Collegiate was a new school with plans of adding a grade level each year. At the time that I was employed there, they only had grades six through eight.

My teaching career was moderately successful, but I had little to no classroom management skills. The only formula I had was that of Zebedee Jones. I would bang on the piano and act just like him, and the kids would sometimes laugh. The music program at Collegiate was brand new and almost grassroots. In addition to teaching general music and choir, I also led chapel services each week.

Even though they were middle school students, I demanded excellence. I ordered tuxedos and gowns for them, and many of them had never had this experience. The music repertoire I selected was quite advanced for middle school students. I took them on a tour, and we would perform concerts for Christmas and spring of each year.

My teaching career came to an end when I received a phone call from Dr. John D. Fuller from Lewis Chapel. He shared with me that he wanted to build his music ministry, and he wanted me to relocate to Fayetteville, North Carolina, to become his full-time Minister of Music. At this point, I was well invested in the students at Collegiate and just couldn't see myself leaving. We were at the end of a school year, and I needed to make a fast decision. I spoke with Mr. Jones about it, and he advised me not to take the job. He didn't think the salary was worth the move. I prayed and followed my heart, resigned from the Collegiate School of Memphis and Antioch Baptist, and relocated to Fayetteville, North Carolina.

On June 14, 2010, I left Memphis and started the twelve-hour drive to Fayetteville. I arrived in Fayetteville and was instructed not to come by the church. It was my understanding that I would be introduced as the new Minister of Music at the upcoming Annual Church Business Meeting, which was two weeks away. When I arrived at the meeting, I was instructed to sit on the very back row, and that Dr. Fuller would ask for me to speak at some point. I received an agenda and sat down. During the meeting, I looked around the church and thought, "Wow! There are lots of people here." Dr. Fuller conducted the meeting in such a professional manner, using Robert's Rules of Order. I had never seen a church operate in such a manner. Dr. Fuller had a heavy voice with a slow southern drawl. He was a well-educated and highly respected man, and from the beginning, I knew that I had to be on my p's and q's.

After the meeting, I slowly acclimated myself to Dr. Fuller's expectations. Lewis Chapel is a large ministry with 4,500 members, four choirs, an orchestra, a praise team, and dance ministries that all fall under the umbrella of the music ministry. In the early days of my tenure, I taught and directed all of the choirs, including the praise team. There were rehearsals every night of the week, and the choir that was preparing to sing on Sunday would rehearse during the week and come back on Saturday morning for a final rehearsal.

Finally, the choirs began to soar, and Dr. Fuller seemed to be very pleased with the work I was doing. He would call me into his office for yearly performance evaluations and say that he knew I missed home but promised that if I stayed, he would make it worthwhile. And he did!

Dr. Fuller retired in 2016 and passed the baton to Dr. Christopher Stackhouse. I am presently still employed as the full-time Minister of Music for Lewis Chapel, and the music ministry continues to soar.

# SONGWRITING
## AND RECORDING

*"God you are my Inspiration, God you are my
light in darkness,
your love for me ignites my spirit, you inspire me
in every way."
Lyrics from Will Harris's song "My
Inspiration."*

I was introduced to the James Cleveland Gospel Music Workshop of America (GMWA) as a child through its recordings and joined the local GMWA Chapter when I lived in Memphis. During my first year in Fayetteville, I joined the Raleigh-Durham Chapter of the GMWA and decided to submit an original song I had been working on titled "When You Pray." I booked a session with a gentleman named Aaron Carter. Aaron was a typical engineer during the session, ensuring I had what I needed and engineering the session. Afterward, Aaron asked, "You're a really good writer; can I embellish your song a little more with some more instrumentation?" I agreed. When Aaron sent the song back, it exceeded my expectations. This initial spark led me to write more, and before I knew it, I had a full album. I named the album "He Knows My Name," inspired by Psalm 139. Though I never had an opportunity to know my biological father, I titled the album "He Knows My Name" as a symbolic expression that God made me, and God was my father. Unfortunately, the album was my first, and after a few years, the perfectionist in me removed it from all digital platforms.

As I was preparing to release the album, I realized I had no singers for the release concert. I had sung soprano, alto, and tenor on the album but hadn't considered how to perform the music live. My desire for my own choir, akin to the Hawkins Family and the Richard Smallwood Singers, led to the founding of Will Harris and Friends in 2013. The choir comprises music educators and worship leaders from North Carolina and across the country. We have recorded three full albums, a Christmas EP, and a few singles, featuring artists I always dreamed of working with, including Chrystal Rucker and Sheri Jones Moffett. Fayetteville proved to be fertile ground for my success as a writer and artist, offering the opportunity to work with one of the world's greatest producers, Maurice Rogers.

Maurice was pivotal in elevating my music, with years of experience working with top gospel artists. His influence is evident on my Christmas album. After being introduced to the Broadway Inspirational Voices, I fell in love with a song by Michael McElroy and Joseph Joubert. I obtained permission from McElroy to record my version of his arrangement of "Noel," which Maurice masterfully re-created to suit my group of singers.

Songwriting has been therapeutic for me. I am a spontaneous writer, drawing great inspiration from Richard Smallwood and Kurt Carr. In the early days, I struggled as an artist, paying my first group of singers, which eventually took a toll on me financially and mentally. Watching promoters pay big names in gospel music while expecting me to perform for free was disheartening. Often, I wasn't invited at all. Initially, I took bookings and paid musicians out of my pocket for exposure. Any honorarium I did receive went to my musicians and singers. Leading the ministry came with many highs and lows, requiring numerous sacrifices. Once, a church contacted me for ministry, but the deacons were upset when I mentioned an honorarium. Later, I learned they questioned my origins, asking, "Isn't he from Mississippi?" This was baffling to me.

The music industry can be very challenging, and as an independent artist, I found myself immersed in the hype of all the glamor and award shows. To be honest, I was just excited that anyone would recognize my music and nominate me. Unfortunately, some of these experiences came with a high and heavy cost. I was spending thousands of dollars trying to shop my music, hire radio promoters, and pay singers and musicians to accompany me when I would be invited places. Eventually, I had to make difficult decisions and learned to re-prioritize. There is nothing wrong with having a dream, but I learned the importance of re-prioritizing my dream. After many years of being an independent artist, my dream wasn't lucrative. I was spending way more money out of my pocket to move my ministry than I was gaining. It had become draining physically, financially, and mentally.

One of the greatest lessons I have learned is not to mimic any other artist. I am confident in how God uses my gifts to bless His people. The doors that are supposed to open for my ministry will open. Becoming aware of my authentic self as an artist has taken some time. It is easy to start comparing yourself to others in this industry, and in many instances, the "entertainment" aspect can be the deciding factor with whether you're invited or not. I have learned to refocus and ask myself the difficult questions. Are you more interested in becoming famous, or are you interested in making Jesus' name famous? The hard truth is I would like both, but at the end of the day, God's purpose for my ministry is to introduce Him to those who don't know Him. Creating a healthy balance for both has been challenging, but I have learned to master it.

Over the years, I have been blessed to present my original music at the Gospel Music Workshop of America and the Thomas Dorsey National Convention of Gospel Choirs and

Choruses. These opportunities have allowed me to meet some amazing music ministers and artists around the world. Recently, I was invited to the campus of Yale University to participate in the Interdisciplinary Sacred Music Program, where I served on a panel discussion and performed in an evening of music. This was a life-changing experience and confirmed that God can make the impossible possible if we just believe. I have learned to surround myself with like-minded, positive musicians who see the bigger picture. No one is an island, and we must learn to support each other. I would have never been invited to Yale had I not joined the local GMWA Chapter and met Dr. Braxton Shelley, who was one of my musicians in the early years for the Raleigh GMWA Chapter. This connection was made many years prior but opened the door for me to be invited to Yale.

# DESTINY

## FAITH IN MOTION

*"All Things are possible, dream big and never let go, faith without works is dead, take one step and he'll make the rest"*

When I began writing this book, I knew I would have to dig deeper into areas of my life that I had completely buried. I have always been very ambitious, and nothing I achieved was ever good enough in my eyes. I realized that I had placed God in a box, only publicly acknowledging the "big blessings" in my life, blind to the small everyday blessings God had given me. It was also difficult for me to see success in any form in my life. I have always been a huge Oprah Winfrey fan, and one day, I listened to her share her definition of success: "Success happens when preparation and opportunity collide." The light bulb instantly came on for me. This has been true in every area of my life. When the opportunity presented itself, I found myself prepared. Initially, when I pondered sharing my story, fear had me paralyzed. I began thinking, who would want to read my story? I haven't achieved that much.

However, through the journey of writing this book, I have learned that gratitude is one of the greatest attributes I can have. I have learned to be grateful for the small things in life. I used to ponder and ask God why He would make it possible for me to be here and be the product of two mentally ill parents. I now understand that when God has work to be done on earth, He makes it possible for you to get here. No one is a mistake. "I am not a mistake."

At one point in my life, I found myself complaining that my career just didn't seem to be flourishing as I had hoped, and then I had an "aha" moment. As a kid, I spent my days on the playground singing songs and waving my arms in front of an imaginary choir. The light bulb came on. This is exactly what God has blessed me to do. Week after week, I get to lead, train, mold, and prepare volunteer singers to worship God through music. Will Harris, the educator, gets to teach, train, and mentor young voices and piano students who aspire to achieve musically. My career in music has been one of the greatest blessings of my life, and it helps to keep me grounded.

As a kid, I would sit in choir rehearsal at North Hopewell Church and watch the adults rehearse. If I am honest, the music ministry was not very good. I could hear them screaming wrong notes, and I wanted to stand before them and teach them how to sing correctly, but I didn't. In the 80s and 90s, there were not many male choir directors, especially in my hometown. If you were a male choir director during my era, you were labeled "soft," and people had no problem hurling demeaning and homophobic slurs. I told myself, I am not going to let them call me those names, so I'll just sit right here and let them "figure it out."

Reflecting on my life in music confirms that I am exactly where God wants me to be. Often, there have been times in my career when I felt that I was just stuck at a red light that would not turn green. Each time I was courageous enough to go down another path, God closed the door. I have learned through those experiences that it is okay to be ambitious and seek higher for your life. When those doors would close, I would find myself in a deep depression, but life has taught me that those closed doors were blessings. I have learned to hear God's voice in a multitude of ways, often through a closed door.

Mom's mental illness and the circumstances surrounding my entire existence fueled an undeniable passion for success. Though I never heard the negative chatter in the community about my existence, I felt it. I assumed that those in my community wouldn't expect much from me. I was just an average student in school, but I knew that education would be the gateway to my success. After graduating from Rust, I pursued a master's in education at Union University in Memphis and eventually completed my master's degree through the University of Phoenix.

Because I was working in church music full time, I felt the desire to learn more about worship and enrolled in a Worship Doctoral Program at The Robert Webber Institute for Worship Studies in Jacksonville, Florida. Webber was an entirely different world for me. At Webber, I was introduced to worship and the arts in a completely different way. We were taught to gain insight from these experiences and consider implementing some of what we learned into our individual worship contexts, but I knew most of what I was learning would be difficult to incorporate into my church setting. Most of the program was virtual, but we were required to attend the campus twice a year for one-week intensive sessions. While on campus, we were required to attend worship at a church completely different from our individual denominations.

During each session, I attended an Anglican Church and was amazed at how everything seemed so connected—the music, the scripture readings, the prayers, and the sermons all seemed intertwined. At Webber, I learned about the four-fold order of worship, the Liturgical Calendar, and the sacred actions of baptism and communion. I was completely enamored with learning about creative scripture presentation. Before attending Webber, I had never heard of a lectionary, and now I consistently use the African American Lectionary when planning music for worship.

The music in our chapel services at Webber was powerful and uplifting. With students from across the globe studying at Webber, I learned so much and have implemented a lot of what I learned in my personal ministry. I am a visual worshiper and have learned to appreciate the beauty of symbolism and creativity in worship. My experience at Webber has undoubtedly been the best worship educational experience of my life. In December of 2022, I received an Honorary Doctorate Degree from the School of the Great Commission Theological Seminary based in Columbia, SC.

Each personal life experience has shaped who I am today. It is my hope that the story of my life will bring hope and healing to those with similar stories. For those who don't have a similar story, it is my prayer that the perseverance and resilience in my life will resonate with you. Mental illness is common in our communities and is not limited to schizophrenia. Many of us feel that we must be "crazy" to seek counseling or therapy. We all need prayer and a good therapist.

My journey of self-discovery has led me to the conclusion that we are all spiritual beings here on earth having a human experience. God's purpose and plan for our lives must be fulfilled before we leave. In my own life, I know I am here on assignment. My mere existence on earth is a miracle, and I don't take the gifts, talents, or the assignment God has given me lightly.

I encourage you to live each day to the fullest, asking God to reveal His true purpose in your life, so you can live out the truest and highest expression of who God intended you to be.

This human experience will bring about some hurts, and if your story is like mine, some of those hurts will be traumatic. It is up to you to begin doing the work towards healing. It is not about the storms of life you will face but how you manage and deal with opposition. I chose to turn my trauma into triumph. The final words in William Ernest Henley's poem "Invictus" have become my mantra, and I have paraphrased it to make it personal: I am the Master of My Fate, and I am truly the Captain of My Soul. Your destiny is waiting! Go get it!

# ABOUT DR. WILL HARRIS

Will Harris is a renowned singer, songwriter, musician, and recording artist. A native of Oxford, Mississippi, Harris began playing piano and singing in church at an early age and assumed his first Minister of Music role at the age of fourteen.

In high school, Harris directed the school's very first ROTC Choir and several community choirs in the Oxford, Mississippi area. While a student at Rust College in Holly Springs, Mississippi, Harris directed the award-winning Baptist Student Union Gospel Choir of Rust College.

In 2010, Mr. Harris relocated to Fayetteville, North Carolina, and assumed the full-time Minister of Music position at the prestigious Lewis Chapel Missionary Baptist Church.

In 2013, Harris founded his award-winning recording choir "Will Harris and Friends," a global music ministry comprised of music educators, worship leaders, and psalmists from the community of Fayetteville and singers from across the United States. Will Harris has composed and performed his music nationally and internationally with the Gospel Music Workshop of America and the National Convention of Gospel Choirs and Choruses. Harris is a multi-award-winning gospel recording artist and the 2022 Dunamis Gospel Award Music of Excellence Recipient.

Harris holds a Bachelor's Degree in Vocal Music from Rust College, a Master's Degree in Education from the University of Phoenix, a Certificate of Worship from the Robert Webber Institute for Worship Studies, and an Honorary Doctorate Degree from the School of the Great Commission Theological Seminary.

facebook.com/will.harris.944

instagram.com/theofficialwillharris

9 781961 475298